THIS
BUSINESS
OF
INTERIOR
DESIGN

THIS BUSINESS OF INTERIOR DESIGN

HARRY SIEGEL, CPA

A Practical Checklist for Analyzing
the Various Conditions of a
Design Project and the Related
Clauses for a Letter of Agreement

WHITNEY LIBRARY OF DESIGN
an imprint of
WATSON-GUPTILL PUBLICATIONS/New York

© 1976 by Whitney Library of Design
First published 1976 in New York by Whitney Library of Design,
an imprint of Watson-Guptill Publications,
a division of Billboard Publications, Inc.,
One Astor Plaza, New York, N.Y. 10036

Manufactured in U.S.A.
Library of Congress Cataloging in Publication Data
First Printing, 1976

To my wife Elaine,
whose devotion and encouragement
enabled me to complete
both this and my first book.

ACKNOWLEDGMENTS

I wish to thank:

Ellen Lehman McCluskey, who insisted that setting forth the analysis of scope of services and related expressions for letters of agreement was a meaningful guide for interior designers.

Albert Siegel, my partner, who over the years has contributed invaluable assistance.

My son, Alan M. Siegel, B.A., J.D., for his invaluable assistance in the preparation of this book.

Jerrold M. Sonet, B.A., L.L.B., my good friend, who has shared the speakers' platform with me on numerous occasions, and who has joined with me over many years in expressing so many of the principles of sound operational methods for interior designers.

CONTENTS

INTRODUCTION

I decided to write this book because, more than ever before, the constantly increasing pressures of conducting business, the side effects of an ever-changing economy, and the challenges of legislative and consumer groups make it imperative that the interior designer recognize and respond to the fact that there is nothing "standard" in a design project.

The purpose of this book is to give the professional interior designer a practical guide and checklist to assist him or her in analyzing, in an orderly fashion, the scope of services to be performed on a given project and the working arrangements under which those services will be provided. In addition, this book provides the examples of words, phrases, sentences, and paragraphs relating to the various conditions of a design project that the designer should set forth in a letter of agreement or a contract.

The scope of interior design services is so broad and varied, and the conditions particular to each job are also so diverse, that unless the designer is aware of the component elements, he or she cannot logically make decisions that affect a fee or compensation base, or construct a letter of agreement, or even decide whether to accept the assignment in the first place.

Frequently, many designers simply proceed on intuition or "this is the way I always do it" basis that can, and often does, result in unpleasant and unfortunate consequences.

I have long felt that in order to eliminate, or reduce to a minimum, the guesswork, intuition, and "by the seat of your pants" decision making, a master list should be developed that itemizes the component elements and conditions in design projects. With such a list, the designer would then have a solid base from which the analysis of scope of services and the related letter of agreement could be developed.

To this end, I first developed the following major category outline:

Opening paragraphs for letter of agreement

Project description

Areas involved

Budget study

Services to be performed

Provisions governing purchases by the designer

Provisions governing purchases by the client

Client responsibilities

Fees and compensation

Retainer

Other applicable provisions

The next step was to analyze each of the major categories and develop a list of check points the designer should be aware of and should consider under given situations in varying design jobs. This became the basis of the checklist on pages 20–26 that includes over eighty subcategories within the major categories.

Because I am aware not only of the business aspects, but of the various problems that may arise from the evolution and completion of the esthetics of a design job, I have consistently maintained that no design job should ever be undertaken without a written contract. Whether in publications, lectures, and seminars for professional meetings or as a college instructor, I always express a strong preference for a well-written individual letter of agreement or a contract written by an attorney, rather than a standard form agreement.

Many interior designers have expressed the feeling that a less formal instrument, such as a letter, rather than a standard form, is certainly more desirable when working in the residential division of interior design. However, such a letter should itemize and set forth all the pertinent conditions and factors of the assignment.

In the nonresidential or contract division, the nature and conditions of assignments vary so tremendously that there is always the possibility that a standard form contract will not provide the language needed to cover all the variations from so-called standard conditions.

Therefore, the designer not only has to be aware of the scope of services and conditions within an assignment, but must also be able to translate these facts into a set of written statements to be incorporated in a letter, contract, or even as additions to a standard form.

Never before has there been available a compendium of phrases or statements that a designer could turn to as a reference to assist him or her in drawing up a series of facts or any given factor needed to define a particular job. Thus, the designer might take the easy way out and copy a previous letter verbatim, or if not, laboriously pull together what he or she thought should be written. Either method can prove unsatisfactory because the designer may run the risk of overlooking pertinent arrangements or stating arrangements in an unclear fashion.

In order to give the designer such a reference work, I have included a series of detailed statements relating to specific items in the checklist.

How to Use the Information in This Book

The checklist is of primary importance, and the reader should first become familiar with its structure and contents.

At the time of initial meetings with clients on a new project, the scope of services and various conditions of the assignment need to be fully discussed and reviewed so that a meeting of the minds can be arrived at. To use the checklist, read through all the categories, and as you go along, check all items that are applicable in the corresponding box. In addition, and by no means less important, as you go through the checklist, pay attention to the items that were not discussed but that might relate to the project itself or to conditions that are relevant.

Thus, the checklist can be the platform from which you can arrive at a realistic overview of the scope of services and conditions.

For those designers who use a standard form contract, the checklist provides a ready guide to indicate conditions that are not covered in the form contract and need to be clarified by an appendage.

After you have completed the checklist, you will have all the basic points that should be included in the letter of agreement, which must then be prepared and signed before you begin working on the project.

It is a known fact that most designers prepare their own letters, and since it is difficult to write up the proper facts based on a stereotyped format, the task of preparing individual letters thus becomes a truly formidable chore. In order to assist the letter writer, I have indexed the checklist with a code reference. The code number relates the specific check point to specific phrases that immediately indicate the type of sentence, paragraph, or word grouping to use in structuring the letter.

In addition, since alternate phrases are included for certain categories, you can pick and choose from the relevant areas once you decide what the particular factors are.

These phrases can also be of assistance in completing the blank spaces of a standard form contract or stating conditions not provided for. The categories and the material included in them are arranged in a sequence that should be the natural order of progression in setting up the letter—beginning with the opening paragraph, the description of services, to the final closing sentence.

Since this book has been deliberately designed as a concise reference source, it does not describe in detail the underlying theories and concepts involved in such subjects as scope of services, initial contacts with clients, and letters of agreement. For a more detailed explanation of these concepts, see my book, *A Guide to Business Principles and Practices for Interior Designers*, specifically chapters 6, 7, 10, 17, and 19 as additional background reading material.

Of course, such a concise book as this cannot possibly cover and spell out every contingency or condition that might develop for any given project. However, when you begin to think in terms of a complete analysis of a job and can refer to the guide, it follows that you will immediately be able to focus on unusual conditions and then deal with them by restructuring a basic provision contained in the book.

Since interior designers work in various esthetic, geographical, and economic areas and with varying personal conditions, the value of this reference book will be enhanced if you constantly add your own individual reference material to the established checklist and provisions as conditions develop and needs arise. For your convenience, duplicate checklist forms have been included on pages 49–64, which can be detached and duplicated to meet your day-to-day needs.

An Example of How to Use This Guide

Here is an example of *basic elements* involved in a project that are developed in initial meetings with a client:

The project involves the design of office space and the specifying of the furnishings and contractors' services.

The client desires to use his own purchasing department to place all orders directly and to have the final decision about the selection of contractors.

The designer's fee will be based on time, with an upset amount.

The client agrees to reimbursement for various expenses and to be responsible for any costs incurred by the designer as a result of the client's specific instructions.

The client agrees to allow the designer to photograph the completed project for the designer's own publicity purposes.

Now, with the checklist as a guide, the designer puts together a detailed list of points to be used in setting up the letter of agreement.

Premises and areas to be designed

Various services to be performed

Determination of functions and design preferences

General design program

Selection of furnishings and materials

Presentation for approval

Finalization of schemes for estimating

Preparation of specification books

Supervision, review, and inspection

Purchasing provisions

Designer to prepare specifications

Client to make purchases directly:
to issue purchase orders
to select contractors
to be responsible for reviewing all bids

Payment to designer if designer makes purchases

Substitutions by client

Sales taxes, delivery expenses, storage, and receiving

Payment for technical services

Design fees and expenses

Base fee

Additional fees for purchases of special orders

Reimbursement for expenses

Reimbursement for renderings

Reimbursement for technical services

Fees for areas not specified

Fees for revisions

Other provisions

Permission for publicity

Retainer

With this outline as a guide, a letter of agreement can be constructed as follows:

Mr. Jonathan Scott, President
XYZ Corporation
650 East 57th Street
New York, New York

Dear Mr. Scott:

This letter will serve to set forth the scope of services to be performed by Jac Shari Interior Design Company in connection with the interior design of your offices at 650 East 57th Street (see Code A-1).

The areas to be designed consist of office space as indicated on drawings supplied by you and include reception areas, executive offices, general office areas and corridors, conference areas and elevator areas (Code A-2).

The services to be rendered in connection with the above areas are as follows:

Phase 1. Preparing the Presentation

Interview executives to establish design preference (Code C-3)

Prepare design program and preliminary layouts for client's review (Code C-2)

Review architectural drawings submitted for any adjustments to proposed scope of work (Code C-4)

Prepare selections of finishes and materials for all new furniture, floor coverings, wall coverings, paint colors, decorative lighting, etc. (Code C-11)

Present the above, including renderings for each area (Code C-17)

Phase 2. Upon Approval of Presentation

Finalize all schemes and decorative treatments

Submit final drawings to various contractors necessary to interpret our design concept

Finalize and prepare specification books of all approved selections for your purchasing department

Prepare design drawings needed for custom furniture and interior architectural woodworking (refer to Code C, phase 2)

Phase 3. During Progress of Work

Review all working drawings, specifications, and finished schedules submitted by contractor to ensure adherence to our design

Approve all materials, finishes, and color samples submitted by contractors

Supervise all decorative work in the field

Inspect all installations at job site (refer to Code C, phase 2)

Purchasing Provisions

We will provide purchasing specifications, schedules, and requisitions for use by your purchasing department, which will handle all purchasing from this point on through delivery and payment. You shall be responsible for issuing all purchase orders, accepting, reviewing all bids, and making final selections of contractors (Code E-1 and E-2).

The designer will have no responsibility for the performance or workmanship of contractors, workrooms, and trade sources selected by and contracted by you (Code E-4).

In the event you cannot purchase directly from your own source and you request that we make such purchases for you, we shall be paid a 15 percent charge for handling such purchases. Such purchases will be made only upon signed approval by you (Code E-5).

You may substitute items set forth in our purchasing specifications in order to purchase directly. However, you must advise us of such changes and substitutions and they may only be made with our approval so that such changes will not materially affect the design concept (Code E-6).

You will be responsible for the payment of all sales taxes where applicable (Code I-1) and all delivery charges and for providing proper storage space and receiving facilities (Code F-9).

If it becomes a requirement of the project that outside engineering, architectural, or other technical services be required for the project, such costs will be billed to you directly. However, no such service will be contracted without your specific approval (Code G-8).

You will provide us with duplicate copies of all vendors' invoices so that we can maintain controls indicating the development of the project (Code E-7).

Design Fees and Expenses

Our design fee for the services outlined above will be computed on the basis of time charges at our hourly rate of three times hourly base pay of the actual time expended by any/all personnel assigned to specific phases of this project. However, it will be contractually understood that an upset fee of $50,000 is set and our fee for time will not exceed this amount.

We shall maintain for your inspection a complete project record of all time expended, and you will be billed monthly based on our time account records (Code G-1).

In addition, we shall bill you monthly for the net cost for blueprinting reproductions, samples, and any out-of-pocket expenses pertaining to this project (Code G-8).

We shall provide two-color renderings and shall be reimbursed for any additional renderings at our net cost of $350 each (Code G-8).

All invoices rendered by the designer to the client are due and payable within 10 days of billing date (Code I-7).

Other Provisions

Any work that we are requested to perform in areas not specified in this agreement will be authorized by you, and written agreement will be made to cover such additional services (Code I-3).

Revisions and changes may be made during the study stage of work. In the event that extra drafting time or other expenses are incurred by us due to changes ordered by you, after your acceptance of original designs and specifications, such expenses will be billable to you at our regular hourly charge plus other costs expended. Such changes or revisions will be made only upon written order by you (Code F-4).

The designer will be permitted to make photographs or other reproductions of the work and to publicly display the same through news media or otherwise, with stated permission from the client to enter the client's premises for the purpose of making such photographs or other reproductions (Code I-5).

A retainer of $5,000 is required upon signing of this agreement and will be applied to the final balance of your account.

In the event that this project is terminated before completion, the above retainer will be used as compensation for services rendered. In the event that the charge for such services is less than the retainer fee, we shall remit the balance to you. In the event that the charge for such services is greater than the retainer, we shall bill you for services rendered based on our time and expense records (Code H-4).

If this agreement meets with your approval, kindly sign and return to us the enclosed copy of this letter, together with your check in the amount specified above (Code I-12).

Very truly yours,

_____

JAC SHARI INTERIOR
DESIGN COMPANY

_____

ACCEPTED

_____

DATE

A OPENING PARAGRAPHS   CODE

☐ Principal aspect and location of job   A-1

☐ Project description and areas involved   A-2

B BUDGET STUDY AND COST ESTIMATES   CODE

☐ Budget study   B-1
☐ Compensation for budget study   B-1
☐ Cost estimates   B-2

C PROFESSIONAL SERVICES TO BE PERFORMED

CODE

☐ Detailed survey and/or analysis of program required — C-1

☐ Preliminary layouts for client's review — C-2

☐ Interview with executives for their requirements — C-3

☐ Floor plans and elevations showing interior architectural changes — C-4

☐ Design firm to consult with architect or other professionals in connection with project — C-5

☐ Client's approval of plans and selections — C-6

☐ Floor plans setting forth furniture layouts — C-7

☐ Layouts and/or specially designed built-in units or other items — C-8

☐ Design firm to submit color schemes, paint samples, fabric swatches, and wood finishes — C-9

☐ Design firm to prepare presentation of purchase recommendations — C-10

☐ Design firm to recommend and submit samples of floor, wall, and ceiling coverings, lighting fixtures, etc. — C-11

☐ Use of existing furnishings — C-12

☐ Design firm to select furniture, furnishings, fabrics, accessories, etc. — C-13

☐ Design firm to supervise contractors' work at job site (painting, flooring, etc.) — C-14

☐ Design firm to supervise contractors' work performed away from site (manufacturer, etc.) — C-15

☐ Design firm's overall responsibility for supervision of all installations on site — C-16

☐ Design firm to present final plans and working drawings — C-17

D PURCHASES MADE BY DESIGNER*   CODE

☐ All furnishings and services to be obtained by designer through
  designer's sources: D-1
☐ Mark-up or billing price for merchandise obtained by designer
☐ Mark-up on contractor's services obtained by designer
☐ Client to sign confirmation of orders and deposits required

☐ Client to sign all contracts for construction directly with contractors   D-2

☐ Purchases made through designer's sources but on client's credit
  and billed directly to client   D-3

☐ Designer to purchase for client as agent (*Important:* for large purchases
  or construction contracts)   D-4

E CLIENTS MAKING THEIR OWN PURCHASES*   CODE

☐ Client to obtain all merchandise and services through own sources   E-1

☐ Designer to prepare specifications; client prepares purchase
  orders   E-1 & E-2

☐ Designer to prepare client's purchase orders   E-3

☐ Designer not responsible for client's purchases   E-4

☐ Designer to purchase where not available to client directly: E-5
☐ Fee for such purchasing
☐ Such purchases on designer's credit
☐ Such purchases on client's credit

☐ Client may change purchase specifications to relate to ability
  to purchase directly   E-6

☐ Obtain duplicate copies of vendor's invoices for control purposes   E-7

☐ Fee or compensation based on client's purchases   E-8

*After reviewing this category, refer to I-6 for clauses about guarantees and
warranties.

F CLIENT RESPONSIBILITIES

- ☐ Designated client representative or liaison — F-1
- ☐ Client to provide full requirements of project — F-2
- ☐ Client to provide drawings, specifications, etc. — F-3
- ☐ Client to pay for revisions and changes — F-4
- ☐ Client to advise of fault, defect, or nonconformance with contract documents — F-5
- ☐ Client to furnish necessary information for progress of work — F-6
- ☐ Arrangement for working funds — F-7
- ☐ Arrangement for working funds with foreign clients — F-8
- ☐ Storage, shipping, and receiving facilities (stress for foreign client) — F-9

G FEES, COMPENSATION, AND EXPENSES   CODE

☐ Budget study fee   B-1

☐ Time charge—no upset amount   G-1

☐ Time charge—upset amount   G-1

☐ Flat fee   G-2

☐ Fee based on purchasing: G-3 (also D-1)
    Percentage mark-up on cost of purchases

☐ Fee based on purchasing: G-4 (also D-1)
    Retail, list, or designer's presented price

☐ Combination of fees: G-5
    Fee for design work plus percentage mark-up on purchases

☐ Complete installation—turnkey   G-6

☐ Square-foot charge   G-7

☐ Billable expenses   G-8

☐ Reimbursement of expenses   G-8

☐ Out-of-pocket expenses   G-8

☐ Shipping, storage, or receiving expenses   G-8

☐ Installation expenses   G-8

☐ Technical services expenses   G-8

☐ Overtime expenses and/or charges   G-8

☐ Billing for renderings   G-8

H RETAINERS

I OTHER PROVISIONS

CODE

☐ Sales tax charge required · I-1

☐ Ownership of designs · I-2

☐ Additional areas not covered by agreement · I-3

☐ Additional compensation for extended period for project completion · I-4

☐ Publicity permission · I-5

☐ Guarantees and/or designer's degree of responsibility · I-6

☐ Guarantee of materials · I-6

☐ Ability to obtain merchandise or services · I-6

☐ Failure of others · I-6

☐ Price changes · I-6

☐ Client payment terms · I-7 (also G-2)

☐ Interest charges for failure to pay bills on time · I-8

☐ Abandonment of project · I-9

☐ Termination of services · I-10 (also H-4)

☐ Arbitration clause · I-11

☐ Acceptance provision: closing sentence · I-12

CLAUSES FOR THE
LETTER OF AGREEMENT

A OPENING PARAGRAPHS

A-1 PRINCIPAL ASPECT AND LOCATION OF JOB

Example 1: The paragraph below can be used when project and areas involved are not extensive.

> This letter will serve to set forth the scope of services to be performed by_____in connection with (a)_____at (b)_____and the terms and conditions of this assignment.

> (a) Insert a description of the principal aspect of the job, i.e., "interior design of your executive offices," "space planning of your general offices," "interior design of your hotel," or "construction and furnishing of your new offices."

> (b) Identify the location of the premises or job site.

Example 2: An alternate opening paragraph can be used when the project description and areas are extensive.

> We are pleased to submit our agreement outlining our proposed work and our terms and conditions as designers and consultants for your new offices (or hotel or restaurant, etc.) at 650 East 57th Street.

This paragraph should be followed by a description of the project and the areas involved (see A-2).

A-2 PROJECT DESCRIPTION AND AREAS INVOLVED

When the scope of the job is extensive and the project description and areas cannot be stated in the first paragraph, then Example 2, the alternate opening paragraph, should be used, and the project is described in the second paragraph.

> **Example 1:** The designer will consult with the client to *ascertain the requirements of the project,* which consist of the following areas:

> > Office space as indicated on architectural drawing #A-7

> > Basement level

> > > Dining areas

> > > Storage areas

> > > Mail areas

Example 2: The area *to be designed* is the office space, as indicated on drawings that will be supplied by the client, and shall consist of:

Reception areas

Elevator foyers

Private offices

Conference complex

As well as any area designated by the client as office space

Note: Examples 1 and 2 are descriptions of a principal aspect of a job:

Example 1 spells out the fact that the designer is limited to consultation

Example 2 spells out the fact that the designer is to design a specific area

The contract writer must be careful (1) to use proper descriptive phrases to indicate the nature of the assignment and (2) to make sure that specific areas are outlined in detail. For a hotel, for example, the description should indicate specific public areas, special suites, number of guest rooms, etc. For an office, the number of private and general offices should be indicated.

B BUDGET STUDY AND COST ESTIMATES

B-1 BUDGET STUDY AND COMPENSATION

If the client requires a budget study as a basic condition before starting the job, then the letter of agreement should state:

> Based upon a review of the above project, the designer will provide a Statement of Probable Costs for the owner's study and approval.

Note: This paragraph should only be included if a budget study *is requested,* and if so, consideration should be given to a fee for this service. If a fee is charged, a sentence should be added:

> Our fee for the preparation of this study will be $_____in addition to any other fee arrangement stated in this contract.

B-2 COST ESTIMATES

If the designer is to prepare and be held responsible for cost estimates, the following is a good statement to include:

> The designer will furnish to or obtain for the client preliminary estimates of the cost of the project. If requested, the designer will review, and if required, revise such estimates from time to time as the preparation of drawings and specifications proceeds. *Definitive costs can only be expected when contract bids are received.*

C PROFESSIONAL SERVICES TO BE PERFORMED

List the various services that are to be rendered to carry through the job. The services should be listed in the order in which they are to be performed. This provides a guide for both the designer and the client. In your letter you can write:

The services to be rendered in connection with the above-mentioned areas will be to:

Prepare floor plans setting forth furniture layouts

Select furniture, furnishings, fabrics, and accessories

Purchase all selected furnishings after approval by client

Supervise installation

If there are numerous services required in an extensive project, then it would be advisable to break them down by phases. The phases should reflect the order in which the job will proceed:

The services to be rendered in connection with the above-mentioned areas will consist of:

Phase 1. Initial review and presentation

B-2 Prepare estimates.

C-1 Prepare a detailed survey and/or analysis of the program.

C-2 Prepare preliminary layouts for client review.

C-3 Interview executives and determine such requirements that may reflect design determination.

C-4 Review architectural drawings and make comments; suggest adjustments to partition layouts and lighting that may necessitate revisions to proposed scope of work.

C-5 Consult with architects and engineers where required.

C-6 Present plans, layouts, and selections for client's approval.

C-7 Prepare floor plans setting forth furniture layouts.

C-8 Prepare layouts and/or specially designed built-in units or other items.

C-9 Prepare design and color studies together with materials and treatments and all information required for the development of the working drawings.

C-10 Prepare presentation of purchase recommendations.

C-11 Recommend and submit samples of floor, wall, and ceiling coverings; lighting fixtures; etc.

C-12   Complete survey of existing usable furnishings, categorizing furnishings for eventual use as well as designated spaces and detailed specifications for refurbishing (refinishing, painting, reupholstering, etc.).

Phase 2.   Upon approval of phase 1, we will:

B-1   Prepare budget costs (if required).

C-7   Prepare detailed layouts.

C-11   Prepare floor covering specifications, etc.

C-13   Finalize the selection of all furniture, draperies, carpet, and other decorative items.

C-14   Supervise work performed by contractors on the site.

C-15   Supervise work away from site, such as specially designed furniture items.

C-16   Supervise installations at job site.

C-17   Prepare final plans, working drawings, and elevations together with details necessary to interpret our design.

D   PURCHASES MADE BY DESIGNER

D-1   ALL FURNISHINGS AND SERVICES OBTAINED THROUGH DESIGNER'S SOURCES

If the designer is doing the purchasing for the client, write:

> We will prepare and submit to you estimates for all items to be purchased on your behalf. Purchase orders will not be issued by us until you return a signed copy of the estimates together with the required 50 percent deposit.

If the letter of agreement does not require a separate fee or compensation paragraph, add to the above paragraph the following, which indicates mark-up or billing price for merchandise obtained by the designer:

> All purchases will be billed to you at list prices, or

> All purchases will be billed to you at cost plus X percent, or

> Purchases of furnishings will be billed to you at cost plus X percent, or

> Contractors and/or any other labor services will be billed at cost plus X percent.

D-2   SIGNING CONTRACTS FOR CONSTRUCTION DIRECTLY

If the client signs contracts for construction directly with the contractors, the letter should read:

> The client shall contract directly with all contractors in connection with the construction and/or building alteration phases of this project, whether or not the designer has obtained the specific contractor.

Such a paragraph is necessary because the designer may wish not to be involved in, or be in a position of being held liable for, uncontrollable responsibilities arising from: acts of the contractor, strikes, inability or unwillingness of the client to meet progress payments, and sales tax problems involving capital improvements.

Note: If the designer's fee is based on purchases and the letter of agreement does not have a separate fee or compensation paragraph, add to the above statement:

> The designer will be entitled to compensation for this phase of the project based upon X percent of the contractor's charges to client.

D-3 PURCHASING THROUGH DESIGNER'S SOURCES, BUT ON CLIENT'S CREDIT AND BILLED DIRECTLY TO CLIENT

The letter should read:

> All purchases of furnishings and services will be specified and ordered through the designer's own sources, but will be purchased in the client's name and on the client's credit. Duplicate copies of all vendor's invoices are to be made available to the designer.

D-4 ACTING AS AGENT FOR CLIENT

The paragraph below is particularly important if the designer is signing for large contracts, either for purchases or for construction work.

> We shall act as agent for the client and shall not be responsible for any malfeasance, neglect, or failure of any contractor or supplier to meet their schedules for completion or to perform their duties and responsibilities under their agreement.

Note: The proper use of the words "acting as agent" and the notice of such to suppliers must be discussed with your attorney for legal clarification.

E CLIENTS MAKING THEIR OWN PURCHASES

E-1 OBTAINING MERCHANDISE AND SERVICES THROUGH OWN SOURCES

We will provide purchasing specifications, schedules, and requisitions for use of your purchasing department, which will handle all purchasing from this point on through delivery and payment. The liability for such purchases shall be the liability of the client and not the designer.

E-2 DESIGNER PREPARES SPECIFICATIONS; CLIENT PREPARES PURCHASE ORDERS

The designer will prepare two (2) complete furniture and furnishings specification books for your purchasing department, and the client will be responsible for issuing all purchase orders, accepting, reviewing all bids, and making final selection of contractors.

E-3 DESIGNER PREPARES CLIENT'S PURCHASE ORDERS

The designer will prepare all purchase orders on the client's own purchase order forms for submission to the client for signature and processing.

E-4 DESIGNER NOT RESPONSIBLE FOR CLIENT'S PURCHASES

The designer will have no responsibility for the performance or workmanship of contractors, workrooms, and trade sources selected and contracted by the client.

E-5 DESIGNER PURCHASES WHERE NOT AVAILABLE TO CLIENT DIRECTLY

Compensation and processing considerations must always be given to how the designer will work with a client. When the designer makes selected purchases (which the client cannot make directly), the following paragraphs outline three situations that can be selected and/or combined to state the facts.

In the event that the client cannot purchase directly from his own source or a source indicated by the designer, and the designer makes the purchase for the client, then the designer shall be paid an X percent fee on such purchases. Such purchases will be made only upon the signed approval of the client.

In the event the client cannot purchase directly from his own sources and requests the designer to issue the purchase orders on the designer's credit, then estimates will be submitted to the client for approval and will require a 50 percent deposit before the order is placed, with the balance due upon receipt of the vendor's invoices.

In the event the client cannot purchase directly from his own sources and requests the designer to issue purchase orders, the designer will do so solely upon the client's credit. The designer will act as agent for the client and the purchase orders will so indicate.

E-6 CLIENT MAY CHANGE SPECIFICATIONS IN ORDER TO PURCHASE DIRECTLY

The client may substitute items set forth in the designer's purchase specifications in order to purchase directly. However, the client must advise the designer of such changes or substitutions, which may only be made with the designer's approval.

E-7 OBTAINING DUPLICATE COPIES OF VENDOR'S INVOICES

The client will provide duplicate copies of all vendor's invoices so that the designer can maintain controls indicating the development of the project.

E-8 FEE BASED ON CLIENT'S PURCHASES

The fee for our services will be X percent of the purchases and all contractors' services specified for the project. Duplicate copies of the vendors' invoices must be provided to the designer.

F   CLIENT RESPONSIBILITIES

F-1   DESIGNATED CLIENT LIAISON

The client shall designate, when necessary, a representative authorized to act in his behalf with respect to the project. The client or his representative will examine documents submitted by the designer and render decisions pertaining hereto promptly, to avoid unreasonable delay in the progress of the designer's work.

F-2   PROVIDING FULL REQUIREMENTS OF PROJECT

The client will provide full information regarding his requirements for the project.

F-3   PROVIDING ALL NECESSARY DRAWINGS, ETC.

The drawings, specifications, information, surveys, and reports pertaining to the base areas will be furnished at the client's expense, and the designer will be entitled to rely upon the accuracy and completeness thereof.

F-4   PAYMENT FOR REVISIONS AND CHANGES

Revisions and changes may be made during the study stage of the work. Changes that must be made by the designer, resulting from revised ideas, structural or mechanical, after the work of the designer has been completed and accepted, will be billed to the client at our regular hourly rates plus any other specific costs incurred. Such changes or revisions will be made only upon receipt of a written order from the client.

F-5   NOTIFICATION OF NONCOMPLIANCE WITH CONTRACT DOCUMENTS

If the client observes or otherwise becomes aware of any fault or defect in the project or nonconformance with the contract documents, he will give prompt written notice thereof to the designer.

F-6   PROVIDING PROGRESS REPORTS

The client will furnish information required of him as expeditiously as necessary for the orderly progress of the work.

F-7 ARRANGEMENT FOR WORKING FUNDS

The client will provide and maintain working funds for the designer as required to pay invoices charged to the project for materials and furnishings, to secure cash discounts, and to pay for required deposits.

F-8 ARRANGEMENT FOR WORKING FUNDS WITH FOREIGN CLIENTS

The client will provide funds to be held in escrow by a United States bank from which the designer is to be paid upon presentation of documentary evidence that delivery has been made to the authorized shipper or shipping area. All payments are to be made in United States currency.

Note: Substitution of identified escrow agent must be made depending upon the client's banking facilities or local representative.

F-9 STORAGE, SHIPPING, AND RECEIVING FACILITIES

The client will be responsible for providing proper storage space and receiving all items of furnishings.

An alternate phrase is:

The client will provide a suitable space for receipt, inspection, and storage of materials and equipment.

G FEES, COMPENSATION, AND EXPENSES

G-1 DESIGN FEE BASED ON TIME CHARGES

The design fee will be computed on the basis of time charges, which are based on our hourly rate of three times hourly base pay of the actual time expended by any/all personnel assigned to specific phases of this project.

We will bill you monthly for all time charges and any billable expenses incurred during each month.

We will maintain for your inspection a complete project record of all time expended.

If there is an *upset* amount to be charged, add:

It shall be contractually understood that an upset design fee of $_____is set and our fee for time will not exceed this amount.

Note: See Codes D and E to cover a percentage charge for purchases made by the designer for the client.

G-2 FLAT FEE

Our fee for the services outlined above will be $_____, payable as follows:

Example 1

20 percent on signing of this agreement

20 percent on the approval of design drawings

20 percent on the completion of working drawings

10 percent on the preparation of purchase orders (or purchases)

10 percent as requested during the progress of construction and installation

20 percent upon installation

Example 2: $20,000 fee

$5,000 on signing of this agreement

$5,000 on acceptance of the final plans and specifications

$5,000 upon the major completion of purchase orders or purchase specifications

$5,000 upon installation

Example 3: Payments for services will be made monthly based upon the services performed within the following phases:

Programming phase: to 20 percent of total fee

Space planning phase: to 40 percent of total fee

Design development phase: to 60 percent of total fee

Procurement phase: to 80 percent of total fee

Installation phase: to 100 percent of total fee

Note: See Codes D and E to cover a percentage charge for purchases made by the designer for the client.

G-3 FEE BASED ON PURCHASING—COST PLUS

Our fee for the services outlined above will be based upon a X percent mark-up on the cost of all items purchased or contracted for you. In the event that you make purchases directly from your own sources, as a result of plans and/or specifications made by our office, we shall receive a X percent fee based upon your cost of such items.

If it is necessary to define cost, then select the appropriate phrase from the following paragraph:

Define the meaning of "cost" and specification of the amount the designer is to receive in addition to such cost on each item. For example, cost may be the designer's wholesale trade price, actual charge to client where client is responsible for purchases, or an amount comprised of designer's wholesale trade price plus a percentage reflecting overhead expense. Designer's percentage compensation may vary depending upon the type of item involved. For example, different percentages might be applied to merchandise readily available from usual sources, as opposed to items specially manufactured or constructed in accordance with designer's plan.

G-4 FEE BASED ON PURCHASING—RETAIL, LIST, OR DESIGNER'S PRESENTED PRICE

If compensation is based on retail and the client requires a definition of retail, then retail should be defined as:

Retail prices will mean: supplier's list price or designer's presented price where special orders or contractor's work is involved.

G-5 COMBINATION OF FEES

Many contracts will be entered into with more than one fee base. In that event, the fee structure can be defined as follows:

Our fee for the above services shall be as follows:

A design fee of $_____ for the development of the design concept and services outlined under phase 1 of this agreement.

Time charges based upon our hourly rates (see phrasing G-1) for all services rendered under phase 2 (with or without an upset amount).

Purchases made on your behalf will be billed to you at cost plus X percent.

Note: Refer to Code C for the use of phases.

G-6 COMPLETE INSTALLATION—TURNKEY

The designer will develop the design concept, layouts, specifications, and preparation of a total estimate, which will be presented to the client for approval. Upon approval by the client, the designer will purchase all furnishings and services required for the project and proceed to installation. The total price to the client is $_____ .

It is understood that after the client has approved the presentation, no changes or substitutions—in either concept or furnishings—may be made by the client without the specific approval of the designer, and the client will bear the additional costs arising from such changes as an addition to the fixed price stated above.

The designer reserves the right to make substitutions in the event that specified items cannot be obtained as a result of circumstances beyond the designer's control.

Note: For payment schedule, refer to examples in G-2.

G-7 SQUARE-FOOT CHARGE

The designer's compensation for the services outlined in this letter will be a fixed fee amount equal to $_____ per square foot of the gross building area of the project. For this contract, the fixed fee is $_____ .

G-8 BILLABLE EXPENSES

The designer will bill monthly for reimbursement for the net cost of blueprinting, reproduction, traveling and subsistence, telephone calls, and other out-of-pocket expenses.

The designer will be reimbursed for any expense incurred in shipping, storage, receiving, or installation incurred in connection with the project.

If it becomes a requirement of the project that outside engineering, architectural, or other technical services are required, such costs will be billed to you directly. However, no such service will be contracted without your specific authorization.

In the event that overtime work by the personnel of the designer becomes necessary, the client will authorize the designer to incur such additional costs and the client will reimburse the designer for such higher than regular rates.

The designer shall bill separately for all renderings requested by the client at designer's net cost.

An alternate phrasing is

The designer will provide X number of color renderings, and in the event the client requires more than X number of renderings, the additional renderings will be billed at our cost.

H RETAINERS

H-1 RETAINER REQUIRED; APPLIED TO REDUCTION OF OVERALL CHARGES

A retainer of $_____ is required upon the signing of this letter and will be applied to the final balance of your account.

An alternate phrasing is

A retainer of $_____ is required upon the signing of this letter and will be refundable upon completion of the project.

H-2 RETAINER AS A DESIGN FEE; NONREFUNDABLE TO EXTENT OF DESIGNER'S SERVICES

A retainer of $_____ is required upon the signing of this letter and is to be considered as payment for the initial study and planning of the project (in the event the project is cancelled by the client during the study stages).

Note: The words in parentheses added after "project" should be eliminated if the retainer is to be kept by the designer in total.

H-3 RETAINER AND COMMENCEMENT OF SERVICES

A retainer fee of $_____ is required upon signing this letter and design services will commence upon receipt of final construction drawings, i.e., room layouts and details, electricity, air conditioning, TV and communications, typical window elevations, and detailed schedule of finishes and materials, etc. This office is to be notified of any and all revisions to above drawings. In the event that revisions are received after your approval of final layouts and necessitate redesign, we [insert name of interior design firm] will be entitled to additional compensation, based upon our hourly cost or other specific costs incurred.

H-4 RETAINER, COMMENCEMENT, AND TERMINATION OF SERVICES COMBINED

A retainer of $5,000 is required upon signing this letter of agreement. In the event that this project is terminated before completion, the above retainer will be used as compensation for services rendered. In the event that the charge for such services is less than the retainer fee, we shall remit the balance to you. In the event that the charge for such services is greater than the retainer, we shall bill you for services rendered based upon our time and expense records.

I OTHER PROVISIONS

I-1 SALES TAXES

It is understood that the client will be responsible for sales taxes where applicable.

I-2 OWNERSHIP OF DESIGNS

Designs, drawing presentations, and renderings as instruments of service will remain the property of the designer whether the project for which they were made is executed or not. They are not to be used by the client on other projects or extensions to this project except by agreement with appropriate compensation to the designer.

I-3 AREAS NOT COVERED BY AGREEMENT

Any work that the designer is requested to perform in areas not specified in this agreement will be authorized by the client in writing and will be charged to the client at our regular hourly billing rates or at a predetermined fee.

I-4 EXTENDED PERIODS FOR COMPLETION

In the event that the time needed to expedite this project extends beyond 12 (or 18) months from the date of signing this agreement, the designer will be entitled to additional compensation based upon the changes in the various cost elements.

I-5 PUBLICITY PERMISSION

The designer will be permitted to make photographs or other reproductions of the work, or any portion thereof, and to publicly display the same through news media or otherwise, with stated permission from the client to enter the client's premises for the purpose of making such photographs or other reproductions.

I-6   GUARANTEES

The designer does not guarantee any fabric, material, or article against wearing, fading, or latent defect, but to the extent permitted by law, client will have benefit at client's sole expense in the assertion thereof of all guarantees and warranties possessed by designer against suppliers and manufacturers.

Furnishing or installing of any or all materials or articles is subject to designer's ability to obtain the same and to procure the necessary labor therefor, and is contingent on strikes, accidents, or other causes beyond designer's control.

Designer will not be responsible for the failure of others to meet commitments or for any other reason beyond designer's control.

Designer will not be responsible to complete a specific order if the supplier's price changes before the order is placed by the designer, provided that the order will be completed if the client reconfirms order at the revised price.

I-7   PAYMENT DATES

All invoices rendered by the designer to the client are due and payable within 10 days of billing date unless specifically stated otherwise in this agreement.

An alternate wording is

Balances due from client (over deposits) for each item of furnishings or service are payable upon presentation of invoices after delivery (or installation).

An alternate wording is

Balances due from client (over deposits) for each item of furnishings or service are payable upon completion by the trade source and before delivery.

I-8   INTEREST CHARGES FOR FAILURE TO PAY BILLS ON TIME

Payments that are not made on time will bear interest at the current rate being charged by local banking institutions commencing 40 days after the date of billing.

I-9   ABANDONMENT OR SUSPENSION OF PROJECT

If the project is suspended for more than 3 months or abandoned in whole or in part, the designer will be paid his compensation for services performed prior to receipt of written notice from the client of such suspension or abandonment, together with reimbursable expenses then due.

I-10   TERMINATION OF SERVICES

This agreement may be terminated by either party upon written notice should there be substantial nonperformance by a party to this agreement. In event of termination due to the fault of the client, the designer will be paid for all services rendered to the date of termination.

I-11   ARBITRATION CLAUSE

Any controversy or claim arising out of or relating to this agreement, or the breach thereof, will be settled by arbitration in accordance with the rules of the American Arbitration Association, and judgment by the arbitrator may be entered in any court having jurisdiction thereof.

Any demand for settlement of a controversy or claim will be made within a reasonable time.

I-12   ACCEPTANCE PROVISION: CLOSING SENTENCE

If the agreement meets with your approval, kindly sign and return the enclosed copy of this letter together with your check in the amount specified above.

INDEX

DUPLICATE CHECKLIST FORMS

A OPENING PARAGRAPHS   CODE

☐ Principal aspect and location of job   A-1

☐ Project description and areas involved   A-2

B BUDGET STUDY AND COST ESTIMATES   CODE

☐ Budget study   B-1
☐ Compensation for budget study   B-1
☐ Cost estimates   B-2

C PROFESSIONAL SERVICES TO BE PERFORMED

CODE

☐ Detailed survey and/or analysis of program required — C-1

☐ Preliminary layouts for client's review — C-2

☐ Interview with executives for their requirements — C-3

☐ Floor plans and elevations showing interior architectural changes — C-4

☐ Design firm to consult with architect or other professionals in connection with project — C-5

☐ Client's approval of plans and selections — C-6

☐ Floor plans setting forth furniture layouts — C-7

☐ Layouts and/or specially designed built-in units or other items — C-8

☐ Design firm to submit color schemes, paint samples, fabric swatches, and wood finishes — C-9

☐ Design firm to prepare presentation of purchase recommendations — C-10

☐ Design firm to recommend and submit samples of floor, wall, and ceiling coverings, lighting fixtures, etc. — C-11

☐ Use of existing furnishings — C-12

☐ Design firm to select furniture, furnishings, fabrics, accessories, etc. — C-13

☐ Design firm to supervise contractors' work at job site (painting, flooring, etc.) — C-14

☐ Design firm to supervise contractors' work performed away from site (manufacturer, etc.) — C-15

☐ Design firm's overall responsibility for supervision of all installations on site — C-16

☐ Design firm to present final plans and working drawings — C-17

D PURCHASES MADE BY DESIGNER*   CODE

☐ All furnishings and services to be obtained by designer through
  designer's sources: D-1
☐ Mark-up or billing price for merchandise obtained by designer
☐ Mark-up on contractor's services obtained by designer
☐ Client to sign confirmation of orders and deposits required

☐ Client to sign all contracts for construction directly with contractors   D-2

☐ Purchases made through designer's sources but on client's credit
  and billed directly to client   D-3

☐ Designer to purchase for client as agent (*Important:* for large purchases
  or construction contracts)   D-4

E CLIENTS MAKING THEIR OWN PURCHASES*   CODE

☐ Client to obtain all merchandise and services through own sources   E-1

☐ Designer to prepare specifications; client prepares purchase
  orders   E-1 & E-2

☐ Designer to prepare client's purchase orders   E-3

☐ Designer not responsible for client's purchases   E-4

☐ Designer to purchase where not available to client directly: E-5
☐ Fee for such purchasing
☐ Such purchases on designer's credit
☐ Such purchases on client's credit

☐ Client may change purchase specifications to relate to ability
  to purchase directly   E-6

☐ Obtain duplicate copies of vendor's invoices for control purposes   E-7

☐ Fee or compensation based on client's purchases   E-8

*After reviewing this category, refer to I-6 for clauses about guarantees and
warranties.

F CLIENT RESPONSIBILITIES   CODE

- ☐ Designated client representative or liaison   F-1
- ☐ Client to provide full requirements of project   F-2
- ☐ Client to provide drawings, specifications, etc.   F-3
- ☐ Client to pay for revisions and changes   F-4
- ☐ Client to advise of fault, defect, or nonconformance with
  contract documents   F-5
- ☐ Client to furnish necessary information for progress of work   F-6
- ☐ Arrangement for working funds   F-7
- ☐ Arrangement for working funds with foreign clients   F-8
- ☐ Storage, shipping, and receiving facilities (stress for foreign client) F-9

G FEES, COMPENSATION, AND EXPENSES   CODE

- [ ] Budget study fee   B-1
- [ ] Time charge — no upset amount   G-1
- [ ] Time charge — upset amount   G-1
- [ ] Flat fee   G-2
- [ ] Fee based on purchasing: G-3 (also D-1)
  Percentage mark-up on cost of purchases
- [ ] Fee based on purchasing: G-4 (also D-1)
  Retail, list, or designer's presented price
- [ ] Combination of fees: G-5
  Fee for design work plus percentage mark-up on purchases
- [ ] Complete installation — turnkey   G-6
- [ ] Square-foot charge   G-7
- [ ] Billable expenses   G-8
- [ ] Reimbursement of expenses   G-8
- [ ] Out-of-pocket expenses   G-8
- [ ] Shipping, storage, or receiving expenses   G-8
- [ ] Installation expenses   G-8
- [ ] Technical services expenses   G-8
- [ ] Overtime expenses and/or charges   G-8
- [ ] Billing for renderings   G-8

H RETAINERS

I OTHER PROVISIONS   CODE

- [ ] Sales tax charge required   I-1
- [ ] Ownership of designs   I-2
- [ ] Additional areas not covered by agreement   I-3
- [ ] Additional compensation for extended period for project completion   I-4
- [ ] Publicity permission   I-5
- [ ] Guarantees and/or designer's degree of responsibility   I-6
- [ ] Guarantee of materials   I-6
- [ ] Ability to obtain merchandise or services   I-6
- [ ] Failure of others   I-6
- [ ] Price changes   I-6
- [ ] Client payment terms   I-7 (also G-2)
- [ ] Interest charges for failure to pay bills on time   I-8
- [ ] Abandonment of project   I-9
- [ ] Termination of services   I-10 (also H-4)
- [ ] Arbitration clause   I-11
- [ ] Acceptance provision: closing sentence   I-12